PRAISE FOR
BERCEUSE PARISH

In his first book, Burnside Soleil inhabits a myth that is almost real, of family, of friends, living and departed, and of the Acadian culture in Louisiana. Soleil's brilliant, close-grained and perfectly worded lyrical portraits are enlarged by the historical and cultural context of a second curatorial narrator, Gus Babineaux. Soleil's transcendent accomplishment is to break the heart and restore it to laughter with redemptive irony. Look elsewhere for promise. *Berceuse Parish* is all there now, and it is a masterwork.

—RODNEY JONES, author of *Alabama* and *Elegy for the Southern Drawl*

Berceuse Parish is an instant classic. Funny, tender, profound, and absolutely goddamn brilliant—here are poems to study and love, lines that will charm you and leave a resounding ache. Burnside Soleil has created a piece of literature that has everything I love about a great book of poems, plus many things I love about a great novel. I can't think of the last time I encountered a poetry collection that felt, on the whole, this originally conceived and winsomely rendered. I want to thrust this gift of a book into the hands of everyone I know.

—GABRIELLE BATES, author of *Judas Goat*

BERCEUSE PARISH

THE BERCEUSE INTERNATIONAL YOUTH LEAGUE & THE ST. HERMÉNÉGILDE SOCIETY FOR GENERAL UPKEEP & SOCIAL BENEFACTION PRESENTS A MELANCHOLIC FANTASIA IN THE TRADITION OF LONELY SWAMP POP, A COLLAGE OF THE CULTURE & PECULIAR HISTORY OF OUR PARISH AS FIGURED IN THE TRAGICOMIC SOLEIL FAMILY, ESPECIALLY OUR UNOFFICIAL TOWN POET LAUREATE, BURNSIDE SOLEIL, IN CONJUNCTION WITH GUS BABINEAUX, AN HISTORIAN OF DUBIOUS ORIGINS & COMPILER OF THIS FINE BOOK, BERCEUSE PARISH.

POEMS

BURNSIDE SOLEIL

THE SABINE SERIES IN LITERATURE, NO. 13

TRP: The University Press of SHSU
Huntsville, Texas 77341

Library of Congress Cataloging-in-Publication Data

Names: Soleil, Burnside, 1983- author
Title: The Berceuse International Youth League & The St. Herménégilde Society for General Upkeep & Social Benefaction presents a melancholic fantasia in the tradition of lonely swamp pop, a collage of the culture & peculiar history of our parish as figured in the tragicomic Soleil Family, especially our unofficial town Poet Laureate, Burnside Soleil, in conjunction with Gus Babineaux, an historian of dubious origins & compiler of this fine book, Berceuse Parish : poems
Other titles: Berceuse Parish | Sabine series in literature no. 13.
Description: First edition. | Huntsville : TRP: The University Press of SHSU, [2026] | Series: The Sabine series in literature ; no. 13 | "The Berceuse International Youth League & The St. Herménégilde Society for General Upkeep & Social Benefaction Presents A Melancholic Fantasia in the Tradition of Lonely Swamp Pop, a Collage of the Culture & Peculiar History of Our Parish as Figured in the Tragicomic Soleil Family, Especially Our Unofficial Town Poet Laureate, Burnside Soleil, in Conjunction with Gus Babineaux, an Historian of Dubious Origins & Compiler of This Fine Book, Berceuse Parish."--ECIP cover.
Identifiers: LCCN 2025036512 (print) | LCCN 2025036513 (ebook) | ISBN 9781680034547 trade paperback | ISBN 9781680034554 ebook
Subjects: LCSH: Soleil, Burnside, 1983---Friends and associates--Poetry | Families--Poetry | Louisiana--Poetry | LCGFT: Poetry | Epistolary poetry
Classification: LCC PS3619.O432526 B47 2026 (print) | LCC PS3619.O432526
(ebook)
LC record available at https://lccn.loc.gov/2025036512
LC ebook record available at https://lccn.loc.gov/2025036513

FIRST EDITION

Author photo by Dr. Shelby MacRae

Cover design by Burnside Soleil
Interior design by Maureen Forys, Happenstance Type-O-Rama

Printed and bound in the United States of America
First Edition Copyright: 2026

TRP: The University Press of SHSU
Huntsville, Texas 77341
texasreviewpress.org

For Rae

Enterrez-moi là où
mon père est enterré.

—TRADITIONAL ACADIAN BALLAD

CONTENTS

PART ONE

PART TWO

PART THREE

PART ONE

La baie est brillante, c'est pas vrai.

—TRADITIONAL ACADIAN BALLAD

Dead Snake Culprits At Large

At approximately 2:00 pm on April 25, two boys dropped a snake corpse on Lester Voisin and Stephen Blanchard. This occurred at Berceuse Bridge where the victims were rowing their boat.

It is believed these boys also stole a bucket of tomatoes from Teresa Blanco.

Parents are advised to bring up their boys in the ways of the Lord.

If anyone has any information, please contact the authorities.

A FEW PARTICULARS ABOUT BERCEUSE PARISH

Berceuse Parish is located between a bayou and a river, Brasseaux and Waxtuygi, and like most settlements in the South is vexed by a history that has little to salvage, except for the century or so of subsistence farmers who lived often enough in collaboration, not conflict, with les indigènes, espagnols, français, gens de couleur libres, et al. During the 19th century, the parish population reached an apex—a modest number, complete with a homegrown abolitionist, Dacpsy Brunet, who converted many townspeople with her evangelical zeal; however, in 1835, les vilains from Broguin torched several establishments, and some homes, threatening the livelihood of many and diminishing the morals of almost all. Dacpsy vanished, presumed dead.

Thereafter, an exodus occurred, though some families remained in the town, also named Berceuse. A local scholar, Augustine Lirette, claims it denotes the second meaning of the word, "rocking chair," not "lullaby." If you tread beyond the grassy fields that a retired literature professor, Pervice Thibodeaux, calls a "heath," then you've left town. A single store, Berceuse Co., and two churches, St. Herménégilde and First Baptist Mission, are the limited but vibrant cultural epicenters. *Le Parlement de Berceuse** almost daily informs its citizens in one of the few remaining bilingual papers in Louisiana, except when it doesn't because Michel Lefrere drank too much the previous night, indisposed at his shack where he will still tell you some news if you knock on the kitchen window and furnish the sill with an offering of whiskey.

—Gus

---

* *Our beloved newspaper name has undergone many iterations, generational rancor about this or that grammatical fidelity to original French or Cajun or cadien. So we've had the Anglophone cadence of Le Berceuse Parlement and others like Le Parlement Berceur, a version helmed by a legendary scholar and poet, Dr. CJ Monier, who accomplished such fine investigative work into the parish sewage system (turns out, it didn't actually exist) before leaving for a post at a fancy university across the ocean. The story of our newspaper's current name exceeds the limits of a footnote, but will feature prominently in a town history to be published next fall by The Berceuse International Youth League.*

CAST

AUGUSTE "GUS" BABINEAUX, *curatorial narrator*
BURNSIDE, *poet (a bit orphic)—his relations listed below*
MARGUERITE or "MAGGIE," *sister (dear)*
JEREMY, *friend (wayward)*
NEL, *cousin (estranged)*
MICAH, *cousin (dead)*
IMANI, *friend (departed)*
HOWARD, *paternal grandfather (checked out)*
NINA, *paternal grandmother (pushing up daisies)*
PENELOPE (PENNY), *mother (astray)*
ULESS, *no-good father (lost)*
CLARA, *ex-wife (first)*
FRANCES, *daughter (surprise)*
MARCEL, *son (another surprise)*
RAE, *beloved (last)*

NEL

Micah was missing again.
It was Easter, a slow spring.
Grandma swept the porch
and said "not one foot."
Sitting on the tractor tire,
we peeled its tread and heard
the chimes made from deer bone—
ribs, jaw, etc.—and on that
evening, it seemed oracular.
Time is when it feels like it.
We wandered to the lake
where people fed old bread
to the gulls, the shoreline
a strepitous scourge of bare
hunger in flight. A boy
almost ran off the wharf,
but someone caught him.
Sometimes, a bird would hover
sculpted by a gust.
When we swim at night,
as we did then, we hold
on to so little, passing
through leaves stippled
in our wake. When my kids
ask what you were like,
I tell them about the plains,
where you moved, how it
once was an inland sea.
I tell them about wild rye
and bluestems—bottlebrush, too.
I tell them how you found
Micah in the dark, digging
hollows beneath the oaks
for two mice he had carried,
all day, in his jacket pocket.

IMANI

You would tell me about *Ulmus alata* and the moths
notched on its twigs. You liked the particular.
I would tell you about the bark cracking the sidewalk,
how a thing can look like a noise. The wood—
it must be dead—mouths *Ganoderma lucidum*,

the conk swilling yellow and orange to an indigo stipe.
Before sunrise, I walk down my street, the light
an alloy of rose and pipe metal. You would pull me
to the yard over there, *Taxodium distichum* in full
frothed leaf, and show how some knees never taper.

If you could still write, you might remind me about
your mother's porch, the paper wasps like pollen
on the comb, the brood swelling white, and how you
cupped and tossed them into the dark of *Buxus*
sempervirens. The petiole still clung to the storm door.

If you could hold *Solanum lycopersicum*, you'd show
how you trellised the vine in your garden, turning heat
into pulp. This might have been the weekend we would
have talked about for years. People, you would tell me,
used to call it something else, a "wolf's peach."

You once wrote that all adjectives are adjacent
to the thing itself. I want to say that when I get
home around 6:00 a.m., I am soaked, clothes puddled,
but under the careful lull of my kitchen bulb, I feel
ponderous, an animal loosed within a sudden forest.

MAGGIE

With a cut milk jug,
you scoop minnows from the bayou.

Glinting, like dimes.

Your white shrimp boots
limpid by the screen door.

It is the languid swell
of the shallows against your ankles.

Grandma calls you back to the porch—
the evening, blue.

You found a floating bag of coleslaw
one time.

Nothing has ever happened.

In the kitchen, a roux—
the tang of home.

The chipped light of the perch swimming.
Your gashed knee scabs.

You are that branch in the current.
A crooked finger bone.
Spring.

What's hunger, you think.
And what's just more?

A FEW PARTICULARS ON THE FRANCOPHONE INHERITANCE

Maggie and Imani were childhood friends, and even though the latter moved away for college, the two girls remained close. Imani first brought Maggie to church, a congregation of a few Black families and some seasonal farm laborers. Imani was a naturalist, attending to the sabbath mostly to appease her parents, but she was foremost in love with material wonders. And she died too soon. I can't deny the elegiac tone of this book.

Michel Lefrere, in mourning, refused to run her obituary, a word whose Latin origin signifies "departure, a going to meet, encounter." He declined all obituaries thereafter, a choice not without antecedent as *Parlement* never published an obit for 15 years at the request of famed resident Stanislaus Étienne Boudreaux—who was the great, great grandpa of our poet.

This venerable ancestor spoke three languages, including French, of course. He was a well known défricheur d'eau, a connoisseur of salt hay, a man who had three children, who loafed sometimes on the sabbath, who then had two children, who watched pigs wander behind homes, who fished at night, a man who (according to legend) thought he had become the moon. And he was a man who loved his wife, Alfredia.

She, unfortunately, died young at sea. Most of the residents were illiterate, but Adonis Lefrere, *Parlement's* then publisher, believed words were an unnecessary sepulcher if Boudreaux forbade friends and family from any public memorial. This story, however, survives.

I cannot tell you everything. I have what's left of that Berceuse. I have the incomplete record, gaps and silences generous enough. I do not know what became of everyone in our cast, not exactly. You may consider this meddling, this constellation of poems and letters and notes and scraps. But I think all things want a pattern. I think all things tend toward a strange order.

Our poet lived here—settled and unsettled, split, divorced, ate, drank, spat, longed, and persisted, and wandered but never really left, never could leave this town.

—Gus

JEREMY

We watched the crows that season,
lonely for a bit of providence.
The heat often dried dozens of worms
on the carport like thin charcoal syllabary.

In the gutter, we found a bird's nest,
pine needles thatched with jute.
The eggs black speckled, mint.
We spared them. It's not the same,

but the next morning, we cracked farm eggs
to fry, yolks colored almost like clementines.
Was there an augury for your sister hitching
a ride with that guy before the summer rains?

In Maine, she raked blueberries,
which she showed us after she returned home
with a daughter. The berry skin seemed frosted
and puckered into a star, the calyx.

She had stories of wheat like bronze feathers,
an island of rock fogged and slick with seals.
In a month, she settled at the sawmill,
working long days as a tender.

Her daughter would often swim in the river,
a gliding cut to the shore. A couple had drowned
there some time back. Pollen, if you let it,
will turn a car's hood to a yellowish fur.

Your sister walked everywhere but would never
leave again. We saw her one evening,
staring. High in the branches a sheet
had blown like a flag or snow.

A FEW PARTICULARS ON COURTSHIP

By the way, you might be looking for more about gumbo or étouffée, or perhaps I've been remiss and haven't chosen poems replete with zydeco and washboard similes and metaphors, whatever kind of cultural kitsch that typically interests the tourist—which is to say, they seek what they can recognize.

Call us Cajuns, or cadiens preferably, or even a slew of other monikers that traffic in stereotypes of lazy, illiterate Francophones contrasted with assiduous and enterprising Anglophones. It's amusing because, for some, they imagine the diaspora as settled and, now, insular, so when I show these collections of writings—Burnside's and others'—to "outsiders," they balk, incredulous. How could these folks travel all around, from Colorado back to the East, when they're supposed to be orbiting only crawfish boils? But we cadiens, we've always traveled. Do you think we know only swamps, not the mountains and rivers and snow? Read a book.

—Gus

CHER PENNY,*

I will be back late. I have left les enfants
chez tes parents. Do not throw out la tarte.
Nor put it in the fridge s'il vous plaît.
I will be back in trois jours.
If Voisin calls or comes by ask him
if his padna still sells les écrevisses
cheap cheap. I will be back.
I ain't going see her. Je te promets.

Ton vaut-rien,†

Uless

* *I include these letters as interludes, the only surviving correspondence between a couple whose fraught relationship complicated the life and destiny of our poet. As you may notice, our poet has pulled an old Robert Lowell and transformed these private correspondences into broken sonnets, tiny love songs that never feel complete.*

† *This term, meant affectionately, translates to something like "good-for-nothing."*

VAUT-RIEN,

I have left all les écrevisses
dans ta chambre à coucher.
Voisin, my ass. Don't come see
les enfants. Mon père has promised
to shoot you, at least les genoux,
if you come by and make tracas.
I hope you get smashed
by a big ass diesel truck.

Love,

Penny

A FEW PARTICULARS ON LIBATIONS

Who lives in this parish of ours? If you can't believe that a mélange of people might congregate along the bayou, that they might have come from the lost colony of Acadie and from the Philippines and from Sicily and from every nation (often cruelly and forcibly), from salt mines and mountain caves, from the desert and Robert Brunet's* 1988 Chevrolet Astro that once hid a granjero pal across the Texas border, then you're a bigot.

That said—Howard, at least what I gather from a few conversations with longtime neighbors, didn't think much of himself beyond his preternatural mechanical abilities and the predominant Acadian ethnicity of his region. His father was born to two Filipino immigrants. Howard opted to pass, unlike his father, and very much unlike his grandpa.

He didn't share too many stories with his children. He pocketed many phrases and cultural practices. He joined the navy. He went to Korea knowing he had no business in Korea, and even though he could spot the island on a map, he didn't have any notion about the place's irreducible complexity. There was the water, a big boat, ink to tattoo his forearm, and men. Men. It's the same story. It's not the same story.

Our poet didn't grow up with the history, and also had scant inheritance with French, a language systematically stymied for decades, so again, always the fusillade against plurality. Uless taught him what he could, but it was tough to do when hitting the road. And Penny?—according to most accounts, she had a fluent knowledge of French, a lilting accent, but she was a wanderer of the local variety, a naturalist or mystic. She kept things private. They weren't neglectful of their own tradition and inheritance, just as Howard wasn't, but it's complicated.

---

* *Robert accomplished a few things, a marvel of a person. He founded Berceuse's first Francophone Gay Rights Organization, but also was an amateur scholar and Xeroxed his slim but impressive volume on the history of Vermeer and light, entitled Vermeer and the Incidental Brightness of the Sea: An Account.*

Only later in life, long after our poet's autodidactic adventures into the history of English nature poetry, did he try his hand at French and discovered, thanks to a lockbox in the attic, his grandpa's lineage. As Howard had passed, our poet couldn't ask any questions, so he sat himself at the library and learned what he could, thanks to old newspapers, all of these quixotic journeys leading to this poem that I'll include as biographically relevant if aesthetically peculiar to our poet's oeuvre:

Howard

You loved to watch nature documentaries—
great horned owls perched in trees, barbed
pinions alert before quiet butchery.
You filched pale figs that Grandma jarred

for Sunday biscuits, your only Eucharist
since a kid when your père brought you
sleepy to mass, but you were used to this:
the cocooned nap in the back pew.

His taloned finger tickled. The banog, he said,
might take your eyes, nest in your skull.
His Philippines was only its eagle, dead
bat slinked in its gray hooked beak, culling

the forest, bleak green pruned to be wilder.
On the shell road, you lagged to lunch,
shocked as he shouted at the steeple, there!
And you rushed, quickened by its clutch.

To be clear, none of this ever happened, or maybe it did happen, maybe exactly, which is improbable, but the world is vast and strange and how underwhelming of us when we pretend otherwise.

—Gus

RAE

You left for San Francisco with your friends,
and I am here—it's not even lunch yet—
wandering through my new neighborhood,

the houses like chrysanthemums, so many
colors, and the blocks speckled sometimes
with blight. I look in one yard, shaded,

tin sculptures of flowers gaudy, all the petals
circular like clocks, and I forgot to tell you
that I looked up your name, which comes

from Old English, something like "dweller
of the willow place." I once saw a Mississippi
Kite slated on a willow, unperturbed

by a mockingbird's churr, screeches operatic
in the sprigs. The northern mockingbird,
I think, means something like "many-tongued

thrush," and this one dashes to the weeds
impasto on the chain-link fence. If I describe
things like this, will you want to come home?

I keep thinking about Walter Inglis Anderson
climbing down tied bed sheets, dangling beneath
some institution's window as he muraled the wall—

birds in flight—with a bar of Ivory soap.
He loved pelicans, as you do, and rowed
to Horn Island, painting them and other

scenes, sometimes his only company a possum.
I would drive you to Ocean Springs right now,
if I could, because I am recalling his mural

at this community center, pelicans aloft near
the window, their bills cerulean and blood orange,
bodies lavender, and the totipalmate feet teal,

or like teal, all of this not decorative but felt.
You would say that the red-orbed eyes
aren't alive enough, and you'd be right,

though you're not here, and aren't these
ornithological changes a clearer vision,
because how many photographs

and paintings have we passed over, their rendering
so precise they disappear—do you know
what I mean? I can't forget the unreal floral

plumage. I can't forget the apricot star-leafed
tree, sinuous bark, the hills or clouds, the dreamy
fauna from a man in love with his loneliness.

But I'm not in love like that.
It was just this morning, the very early morning,
when we said goodbye, the blue touch of your hands.

A FEW PARTICULARS ON THE BERCEUSE DIALECT

In his travels, our poet has been chided for exceeding what others sometimes deem an acceptable provincial dialect, a Francophone glossolalia authentic to the swamp. It is true that our poet's forebears, and even his friends, spoke an idiom more moss than marble, the vocabulary warped by climate, as is the case anywhere, but such was not the case for our scribe, who spent his summers in Ms. Comeaux's library, not exactly public though communal in spirit.

She collected newspapers and periodicals for the old folks, children's books, too, of course, but often purchased—and in one legendary case purloined—Great Books, some of them editions (i.e. Tennyson to Whitman) intended for middle-class subscribers eager to include a bit more cultural cachet on their bookshelves. Few read these tomes, their spines uncracked until our poet arrived. He pored over the books most evenings on Ms. Comeaux's porch, where she also told him about Mahler, Puccini, and Offenbach, her elocution and knowledge astonishing him, so much that he rarely noticed the mosquitoes pestering his ankles.

A retired elementary school teacher, Ms. Comeaux settled into a life that was entirely hers yet incommensurable with the operatic visions of her inner world. Around town, she was mostly known for once forbidding Cécile Bourg from bringing his rooster, Don Louis, to recess. Despite her injunctions against schoolyard fowl, Ms. Comeaux's disposition was generous, and in the big oil bust of the 80s, she aided our poet's family, slipping an envelope with a check for $1,000 to prevent his father from seeking work in the abominable north of this great Gulf state. No one anticipated, however, that Uless would take the money and abscond to Colorado.

—Gus

MARCEL

For a month, I have been living here
and often sit near the back bedroom
wall, mice scuttling behind

the tiny framed self-portrait of Rembrandt,
laughing, skin crinkled like gold leaf.
He's Zeuxis in that one, I think—

Zeuxis and Parrhasius, I remember
the contest between them, how Zeuxis
painted grapes so true—what do I mean here?—

that birds flew down to feed, yet Parrhasius
depicted a curtain concealing his work,
the verisimilitude fooling his competitor.

Yet of the two paintings, I'd most want
to see the grapes, not a curtain, of course,
these grapes clustered purple, reminding

me of walking with Marcel, one or two
blocks away from here, the mulberries
bloodied on the sidewalk. My son—

he gathered in his small hands the fruit
fermenting, this wild sweet melt,
this jam scooped from the ground.

It's true. There were no birds.
About our backyard beech, my father
once told me a lightning bolt singed

the heartwood and pith like a wick.
He blanketed the little fires charring
the sapwood. There were no birds

on the snag for weeks, he said, which
must be untrue. I prefer imagining
the tree swallow in the cavity, and I know

it was summer then, but what if I say
winter? What if I want the swallow's
blue glare? I cannot tell you how to love.

PART TWO

Nous sommes allés dans les bois
pour voir si la lune est tombée.

—TRADITIONAL ACADIAN BALLAD

NEL

You saw him kneeling in his skiff,
one oar jutting like a femur
from mud. That wasn't
the last time you saw your father.

You are still the boy told to go
sleep in that shed, slumped roof
tangled by flowering vines
we call poor man's rope.

Yellow stars in your long night.
That's the one detail you told the woman
you loved in Ohio, where you'd
walk past country cemeteries,

three of them, to Left Fork Camp Creek,
dousing your hair in chilled water,
ice like ribbed vaulting on rock.
You'd both swim, sometimes,

hoping a baptism would take.
She taught you that a river has many
headwaters, but each troubled night,
a single origin called back to you—

years ago in the woods, your father
climbed the sweet gum to find a bee nest
in a hollow, a fermented wound of propolis,
the smell of larvae's honeyed rot.

On a twig, a copper underwing seemed
like a gut unspooled. We tell it now
like an allegory. The tree shuddered
and wouldn't let him down, not in the dark,

and soon we barely saw his boots,
and soon there were only leaves. Soon
it would be cold as geese took flight
from a slim crook of shore.

A FEW PARTICULARS ON KANTIAN DISINTERESTEDNESS

Charlie Three, whose moniker is actually Charles III, wasn't malicious, mostly guilty of narcissistic self-mythologizing, and while he worked just hard enough and loved as he could, which is to say with unremarkable friendly care, he never really moved Maggie, no great declarations of romance or passion or even touch. Theirs was a marriage of other rooms.

A welder who practiced faith healing, Charlie proclaimed his ability to heal rickets, but as so few children suffer any longer from this ailment, he never much summoned his powers.

Charlie Three was rotund, his face perpetually peeling from sunburn, his hair whitening early and yellowing earlier from years dedicated to cigarettes. Maggie never fell in love with him. There wasn't an idyllic past lost to the mundane present of adulthood. Sometimes—if you're old enough, then you know—one simply ends up with someone.

What to do with a life like that? She turned their front yard into a sculpture garden of glass figures, most of them bottles and mason jars, all assembled into angelic figures surviving by silicone. She called them seraphim.

—Gus

MAGGIE

i

Some morning,
long after our mother
has left this world,
you will hear a lady next door,
hanging her dresses to dry,
her singing brittle,
like a cracked vase
or a chipped tooth—

a voice, like our mother's,
tempting,
come back.

ii

You smoke
outside, bonfire
for gnats.

You hear the lilting
brawl of the moon.

Grits
hot in your belly.

You think about a white bowl
of cherries—our grandma:

You know those hands—
song-made, two fingers.
Pirouette.

iii

The cane pants in the flames.
You watch from under the fig tree,
its fruit purpling like contusions.

Perched on the crook of a branch,
a cardinal.

Nearby, a drawbridge.
Boys on it.

A book's cracked spine sheds its pages,
windblown, like little sails beating about.

That night, what could you tell him,
except about the rain bruising through the shutters

and that the termites would swarm soon—
their wings like syllables of light?

JEREMY

We woke on the wooden floor,
and in the corner of the room,
cups of rain—your roof leaking.

Your window framed moss on the oak,
where two hawks landed, ruddy-barred
chests, and we watched and had nowhere

to be, and this morning a single hawk,
young, darker feathers, hushed the electric-
like hum of cicadas in the pine.

It's been twenty years, and the rain
still cools the September air, for now.
Those cups—plastic carnival throws—

you'd fill with flowers, mums purple
and bronze, all plucked from the neighbor's
garden where she kept the dog leashed.

And the ceiling mold was like a watercolor
black sea. You used to like things like that,
mushrooms bracketing a snag.

Childhood is deciduous,
like this evening when two white egrets
plumed in the median, and then one flew

to the bayou, the other nearly into my car.
I pulled over as it landed in the shells
spined along the shore.

Once you kept the names of birds
in a graph notebook.
The summer we were twelve,

you stopped. There were too many.
What we need to understand
each other is often belated.

Time is rain in these trees,
the wrens pitched after lace bugs,
this feast of golden scales.

A FEW PARTICULARS ON PATIO FURNITURE

In Colorado, Uless herded sheep only to be fired once he assisted a local conservation group reintroduce wolves into an area owned and protected by his employer. This is perhaps a book of itinerant fathers.

There's also Nel's father, T-Jean, whose name might seem fictitious and laughable, but you're being insensitive. As I was writing, T-Jean had the inglorious distinction of abandoning his family to farm blackberries in Virginia. Maybe his name is comical. We should note that these blackberries were excessively delicious, the drupelets plump and sweet, an exaggeration of flavor. He would bring buckets of them on his rare drive back to Berceuse, but these were nothing compared to tasting them right off the vine, as Nel did once he, too, fled from our parish to the plains and then the coast.

Micah's father, Jim—his story, brief. He would sit in the woods, a lawn chair usually, and drink all day, sometimes chatting with hunters, most often with Jerry who was an avid forager. Jim liked tall tales, things he'd repeat until all the details were glorious, like the time he allegedly stole and drove a Ford Mustang Shelby GT 350 into a cane field, the vehicle erupting into flames and torching the crop, which he watched incinerate once he escaped all the smoke. He had plenty of excitement, he said, when he was young. He just wanted to sit down for a while and drink.

Hard luck finding a body in the woods. Everyone thought they would, as he never came back after one weekend at his own Walden Pond.

The trouble with Micah had already exploded when Jim did come back, explaining that he had a vision of the archangel Gabriel who forbade him to ever drink again, and as punishment, he had to walk the country preaching God's message. I don't know if Gabriel also instructed his prophet to father two kids in two different states, but it looks like Jim did that, too.

—Gus

RAE

Branches limb the river, which isn't a river—a stream,
a waterfall glutted from rain. We cross, boots soaked,

and why is it so funny, sometimes, when you're
dying almost, or could? On the other side, a woman

stands near a few firs and says we're lucky. I hesitate
to be declarative, but self is the first story told to us.

And what about that which isn't narrative,
a portrait without

beginning or end—fascicles like capillaries
in a body of light?

Tell a story long enough and there goes
your whole life. This day begins my fortieth year,

and I know so little. A century ago, sheepherders
carved the news of their loneliness on aspen,

these very ones. In winter, elk strip the bark
like wafer. But it's autumn, and we're quiet

as if we might startle the golden bands of leaves.
Adulthood is the last magical word.

CHER PENNY,

It ain't that I won't rentrer pas à la maison.
There are just too many choses out here
in Colorado, comme elk. Big & big, wild wild.
I wish you could see em là tu saurais mieux.
It ain't even the same lune. If you were here,
je te donnerais le ciel. Et pluies. Et capot.
I swear on your petite cheville that I love.

Ton vaut-rien,

Uless

VAUT-RIEN,

That night heron a mangé toutes les tartes
car tu n'étais pas ici. I let it. I gave it to others,
too, gratuit, car tu n'étais pas icitte. I cut it and cut it
and gave it to pêcheurs to fermiers to badjos
to la lune to les orages car tu n'étais pas ici.
I will bake the biggest tarte in le monde.
It will fill up ma maison. It will break le plafond.
I will feed the whole rue, quartier, ville,
and il y a des baies et chocolat et pacanes
et everything you could want
and none, none, none for toi.

Love,

Penny

PENNY

The winter you left, it snowed
for the first time in fifteen years,
tree limbs graying as if antique.

Steam sloughed from shingles.
Snow is never snow here, a fable,
pallor on a lawn, and when we rushed

past screen doors into what seemed
like a monochrome film, our skin—
stones in a gulch.

We were artisans packing
flakes to decorate our porch,
globes melting by touch,

and by the afternoon, the figurines
thinned to stalagmites, glass souvenirs.
I watched the frantic adoration

of an hour, the roads slick,
one lonely car tumbled in a ditch.
Busted pipes, especially beneath

raised homes, plunged yards
into streams as a few pilgrims steadied
themselves to morning mass,

some marveling at frost curling
like fronds on window panes.
In polaroids, we looked like plush

dolls in fluffy coats posing
on a clean sheet of paper.
My sister and I, my cousins.

I cleared your old garden of ice,
the stakes bare, pulling white clover
and burweed. You might imagine

us on this day, a reflection that no
object could cast. It's not like
the six miniature sailboats

mirrored in our winter lake.
Six men, on the other shore,
stared, faithful, in the cold.

None of it is really there anymore.
You were my mother. I will forget
the color of your hair, and it's not

like this last tree is about you,
or anyone, or almost like any year,
a sugar maple pouring cherries in frost.

A FEW PARTICULARS ON PARTICULARS

Penny. Penelope. She first learned to read from whiskey bottles. American Beauty. Rye Whiskey. The rye took some practice, of course, but helped later with "eye." "Beauty" and "whiskey" cousined.

She often told the story of crawling beneath her childhood home to prophesy in chalk her death date. She was a lonely child, quiet, alert, someone who would spend hours walking near the bayou or river, who wanted to learn about all the fish without harming a single one. She was a peculiar girl who gave particular names to trees, appellations she wouldn't share with others, only with her children much later.

Only with Uless was she lively, these two raconteurs who'd compete for attention and gabbed about so many stories that the atmosphere of their modest home must have been suffocating with narrative (funny because their letters are so spare, warm—still, all those lost stories). Love doesn't need to live together, which is what Penny once said to our poet. When Uless left, she left, too, the kids spending most of their time with the grandparents, which is how Nel and Micah and our poet bonded. Orphans in all but name.

Penny kept strange hours and was most active after midnight, an ambler of the woods, with a naturalist's eye for flora and fauna but with her own names, always her own names, like green wit and hair-tangled sea bit,* someone probably more in love with sound than sense. She'd make her way through the trees and, on rare occasions, show up at her parents, tapping the window of our poet's room. He would open it just a touch to hear her without letting in all the mosquitoes. She would tell him about the world, a concatenation of things that would never happen again, like the deer's antlers, rain-swept, or the moon white on the leaves, all of these things named secretly, things that our poet wouldn't reveal in his journal.

---

* *A live oak, which I know only because an anonymous source once overheard her explaining the term to our poet. I should perhaps withhold this terminology, but what imaginative fecundity.*

And who knows, in the end, why she left? She pulled a Thoreau, one could argue, and out there in the wilderness, we wonder what truth she found. It's no good to indict, though. What we do, sometimes, is just what we do.

—Gus

FRANCES

That was the day you learned the wind could splinter a pine.
You crawled—even when I told you not to—through the thicket

of toppled branches, and this was the morning when I first noticed
cobwebs silvering the grass, though someone later told me

it was mycelium. And few people believed we saw an owl
on a limb, clawing and jaunting before hurtling into a bush.

Your uncle kept a falcon, or hawk, I can't recall, when he lived
in Vermont, and built a mew for it, a shed, darkened like a cave.

He fed it some days, beggaring it to hunt, the last twitch of mice
in its beak. He liked that God had said no one could eat this bird,

this creature that is hunger, sinewy and lean. When you first crushed
the mouse spider—it was the cool front after the storm—you asked

if it's a mercy to be done and done, and I don't know, though we dug
two graves two weeks apart for the veery and ovenbird, each plunged

into our windows, the one in the front and yours, these two birds that
I thought were the same, bronzed green feathers, almost like pennies

tarnished. Some nights, we sit for dinner, no one talking, the picture
window framing us, and on this night, you make me kneel next

to your new bed, finding the two pillows you need for your neck,
and I tell you about a mutt loose on the levee, how I followed

him past the bricks rooting the hill of the Old Spanish Fort where I saw
an oak husk, its bark brittle eddies. We come so close to things.

The water is cold, and no one body will warm it, not tonight.
I haven't ever stopped thinking about your first snow,

about your front tooth tugged free, about the boat in the lake,
the pilings we saw topped by pelicans, slender as fish hooks.

PART THREE

Triste, mais…

—TRADITIONAL ACADIAN BALLAD

MICAH

I hid in the ditch low by the sedge and tore the white
tendrils of chickweed from the red gut clay Micah
climbed the ash's ribbed bark its panicles
like chimes Grandpa had called us all to work
to hack limbs but we wandered past the cane field
burnt clean and got lost in the forest each tree
every other tree sitting on a stump together its heartwood
a ringed map Micah took pecans from his pockets
cracking and chewing them an impossible slew
of pecans cradled in his arms the crows roost
out here he said my father abandoned me he meant
we had the same language scuffed knees scent
like grass or hay caught in your hair
his black hair always wild taut knots like knuckles
we ran toward a blackberry bush kneeling near its spiny
stems plucking its fruit purpling our fingertips laughing
a feast worn like a mask sweat cooling our backs our hands
the most real part of anyone but you died last week
in prison I cannot even see it the same night my daughter
brought home a seedling hugged in a damp napkin
the green stalk choking the bean the shell flaring like lungs
we hadn't spoken for years but look at this plant that
has nothing to do with you its slender tangle the leaves
wrinkled when I forget to water it's like that time we
fished in the paddle boat and I caught that perch
the whole evening smooth on its coin belly and you said
no throw it back unhook it careful now it's too small
but I kept it and we watched it pant among the ice

NEL

Honey locust and the fishing rod.
Hook silvered creek.

You say a river baptized our grandpa.
And from the canopy of branches,

you step into this purl of rain
to hold a bream like a sheet of copper.

Gods change things all the time.
Your feet into cattails, fingers ox eyes—

tomatoes lipped on spun vines.
Hold one, cut one. Who knew light could do that?

Each summer, you are one chalked fir
snagged on a feral green hill.

The heavy rust rattle of cicadas.
Three hawks in the brush.

If not the moon,
then a word for it.

Who knew what sons we might have in spring?
Mine, the warm glide of his hair.

A FEW PARTICULARS ON THIMBLES

Once, Jeremy cut a cucumber, salting its flesh. There wasn't a burning bush, only a kitchen, with a heap of unwashed dishes, but Jeremy heard the voice of God. Like the pealing of a bell, he said. However, he finished cutting and eating the cucumber, even adding a little pepper.

In the deepest regions of the South, it is unremarkable that someone claims to hear God's voice, like thunder some explain or others describe it as cicadas (this specifically being Ms. Mary, who last September tried to baptize three feral cats in the canal). And still others say it's like the timbre of a father or a mother.

My own grandma, Bertha, used to drive to the Waxtuygi and sit under a certain tupelo where she buried the shoes of her firstborn, and as she would unearth these tokens, God would speak to her, or so she said, but the sound was from the river, the language like stone splitting the stream. She would return home and sit on her rocker, and we'd ask what God told her, if it was anything about the future, about the crops, or something grisly like death and murder. But she was a cryptic old lady. The voice, she explained, only said *listen, listen.* Of course.

I don't know what Jeremy heard, but he followed his father into the ministry. Jeremy was so much concerned about God and the Holy Spirit and Jesus that you could no longer get close to him, crowded by spiritual matters, incessant as gossip. He heard the voice of God and gradually couldn't hear anyone else.

He married, a few kids, three—I believe. On Nel's last night here, before he moved to the plains, he ran into Jeremy at the grocery, the two talking idly of old times, about our poet, too, and how they would climb the trees near the bayou and leap into the water, boy after boy. They were so young, invulnerable, at home in the murk with the minnows and perch, sometimes even the alligator gar. They would leap, and often from the road, someone would call out to them, cheering them on, witnessing, or cautioning them—*watch out*. They didn't always know those voices. You could almost say, if you prefer the imaginary, that those might have been the calls of the minor gods of the woods, trees that had seen so many kids pass through their branches, so many paddling in the water, and it won't always be like that. Summer is really only summer in childhood.

You grow up. Watch out. You grow up, and can't return.

—Gus

JEREMY

When your wife died from pneumonia
last winter, I thought of the sycamore
we climbed in your backyard. The tree's
mottled crust gripped our toes, and from
the lowest branch, we flung our bodies
to the dirt, wondering at the scuffed
archipelagos on our knees.

Dewberries bellied purple along
the chain-link fence. We plucked a few,
spines and bristles ribboning our catch,
and brought handfuls to your mother
who stood at the kitchen window,
a milk jug open—a sour cold.
She had ten years left with your father.

In the finger-grass, we saw sparrows
bobbing like tacks, sweet brown churrs
that lobbed and pecked a lizard,
splitting its gut to reveal something like
a fresh red tongue. I remember our
Saturdays thick with butterweed,
roadside ditches hovering yellow,

and the white clover heedless amid green.
The bees we'd pinch by the wings,
delicately, if we could, admiring
the scramble of thin legs. We'd let go,
and they'd still flit to the next batch
of pollen. And do you recall behind
my grandma's old trailer, that bit of wilderness:

out there, the spectacle of that single duck,
blue-billed, feathers black and white,
but the bill a cynosure? Remember we stared—
all of us maybe—into the snarl of branches
breaking light? It wasn't delicate.
It wasn't a beatitude. It was just one day.
A bell. There aren't enough trees to say this.

A FEW PARTICULARS ON DEUTERONOMY

There was a field, the winter warm and the afternoon fogged. They ran through what seemed a thick cloud, the distant trees rooted in the haze. The boy laughed, chased by the girl. Both laughed when the father chased them. Shoes were kicked off, and there was little else except the sound of them running through the grass. It was almost night, and if we can imagine seeing them from above, they patterned curlicues until exhaustion. They rested on a wooden bridge where water couldn't be seen below. It was the daughter, I think, who noticed first. Then the son was exuberant, as usual. They could see. He could, too. Two pelicans, wings enormous, cut through the murk. They landed and sailed along the bayou, twin ghosts. It all ends in birds, which is what our poet believed. Each ending, different. Each creature its own. Every mythology is private, untranslatable.

They watched together for a while until the father said it was almost time to go home. Not yet, but almost.

—Gus

ULESS

Lichen bristled spruce, thimbleberries near
the last ice. I drank from a stream cured by rock.
I had never seen water like that, clarion,

jugging some for the cabin. Sometimes, I'd wake
and from the window watch a moose chew foliage.
I wondered about mountain lions, about my father

who often slept outside in a tent near an old mining town.
When I looked for him one day, I thought of the argument
that the only thing bigger than a God we imagine is a God

who exists. It doesn't work—or maybe works better—
if we say the only thing bigger than a life we imagine
is a life that exists. I found a boulder rippled by moss,

and rolled from the adit, cragged and wreathed
with more moss. I thought the dark was like a maw,
like a bear, that it was a cave. I wanted it to be a cave.

A FEW PARTICULARS ON PURGATORIO

When Uless got to Colorado and borrowed some hiking boots indefinitely and landed a job as a forest tour guide, despite being unaware of the terrain, he sat—by his own account—on some crag and surveyed the unmitigated majesty of the Good Lord's tremendous work and realized he never should have left his kids.

It takes mountains, sometimes. He lived out there for a spell, leaving and then returning to settle in some snowy enclave, which after postcards and letters and money orders and more he persuaded his children to visit. Maggie liked the mines, our poet the peaks.

When Maggie returned to Berceuse, our poet stayed with his father for a while, earning a few bucks cleaning up a tavern, sometimes talking to Uless late into the night, walking until it was morning. Deer around. Elk.

Our poet wore one coat, and after a while, he, too, picked up the habit of two or three, socks doubled. The night was big, then bigger, and sometimes, there was only silence, except for their boots as they walked back to the cabin. Uless would close the door, and they'd gather near the hearth. There would be a story, usually, something preposterous, and our poet would listen, and there was warmth, and there was drink, and there may have been forgiveness. It wasn't love, but like love, and enough.

—Gus

MAGGIE

You walked on a pelt of leaves to a fence
behind which natural gas plant pipes flared
like a luminous sheath over dark wood.
You've been married since you were eighteen,
lived out of state once during a war,
and the night we decided to stay here
always, we listened to robins tuning
to unnatural light. If it were another
life, you would tell your son—he would be three—
to get back in the car, that there's a cold
front coming, that it might rain again,
which it did, a rain that is here only now.

CHER PENNY,

Marguerite dit que tu es malade. C'est vrai?
Je sus presque là. On va aller dans le bois
ayoù la lune high high, et tu vas massacrer
tes souliers dans la terre et les bâtons.
On boira toute la nuit. La nuit est assez
lumineuse. Tu pourrais rire, mais tu es comme
des champs de bleuets. Je sus presque là.

Ton vaut-rien,

Uless

ULESS,

Je veux pas faire un abus à toi. Le gros bec
était après s'effarder. Écoutez, vaut-rien.
Je veux trop de fleurs. Colorées. Pas de mots
s'il vous plaît. Juste de la lavande, lys,
narcisses rouges, marguerites et roses
white white. Je veux—j'aimerais qu'un
truck te tue. Toujours.

A FEW PARTICULARS ON PULMONOLOGY

But Rae stayed. Everyone would leave, eventually, and it was so much easier for her to go, too, but look at them. It is the morning. In their kitchen, he fries eggs—two for each of them—and after the sourdough is toasted, she butters, careful to gather the crumbs. Their coffee, black, goes into his red mug and hers, white with some worn graphic, a few fir crowns floating in the ceramic sky. The rest must have been a mountain.

—Gus

RAE

I lived my first life wrong,
or much of it, which I realized
crouching in the hollow of a tree,
a "goosepen" some call it,

a place where a hermit once dwelled
with a wood stove chimney'd
through a cracked husk.
Bay laurels ribbed the fogged trail,

roots scalded to stone glyphs.
We watched the redwood bark
plait and then constellate green.
I've sometimes wondered

if I will recognize the end
of things, and if this could be
a study in recognizing my own
end, which isn't to say purpose,

though that, too, must be the meaning.
A doe, later in the foothills, appeared
among oak and ivy that draped
like a baldachin—or we appeared,

and with your boot bleeding your left heel,
you had to keep walking to the shore.
I sat on the trail, though, I'm sorry,
waiting for the deer to decide enough,

which she did, bounding up the path,
but there from the brush, a fawn
crouched and considered the creature
I am—another come down from the peak.

In the one photograph I have
of them, I see now they weren't doe
and fawn but yearlings, their summer
of forbs, ranging hunger hidden

in thickets, not foundlings
within the care of my attention
or my memory. I tell you everything
and will, always, or try,

so they were deer and then just deer
by the time we made it to town,
past all the bleached houses,
and I couldn't

say what had happened, not yet,
so we stood together on that beach
embanked by a cloud where two fishermen
seemed to angle as if for hawks.

A FEW PARTICULARS

My dad, Nicolas Jean Babineaux, once stole a library book about various visual depictions of Hell. He was a small man, intelligent and literate without ever having attended anything beyond high school, a man gifted with an unparalleled ability to be fascinated, to be consumed by some impression or subject or idea, which is what happened late in life with Botticelli's sketches of the *Inferno*.

My dad liked to tell me about this one sketch of Geryon appearing like a trifecta of monsters, which is funny because, of course, Botticelli evokes narrative progression, the agreement tacit that this isn't all happening at the same time. But his limber, detailed lines populate the page—sheepskin, once—with figures like Dante posed among the usurers, and the eye travels like the river down the parchment, but what I'm really saying is that it's not clear that Geryon descends with the poet and pilgrim because the second creature seems to return to the first iteration. Go look. The third and fourth positions plunge into the pit while the ancillary beast,* with its reptilian body and telson that seems alphabetical, could be embarking or disembarking with the pilgrim. I would stare at this illustration at night—what was that room even like?—fruit flies ripe in the air.

He read miraculous Biblical stories as we all bunked in the old houseboat, tales like Jesus feeding thousands from a few fish and some loaves, the scarcity prayed into plenty. We especially liked the dead coming to life again and incessantly asked about decomposition, we grisly believers. It was the default, that the world surged with some peculiar unnamable magic.

I read the same stories back to him in his final weeks. He was happy, despite his lung cancer. Like his favorite Botticelli sketch, he seemed both to be departing and remaining. He told me he liked all those depictions of Hell, some too gruesome, but others beautiful in some terrible kind of way. Think about Francesca and Paolo, like doves in the blast. I'm sure

* *In the Inferno, fraud is the rankest sin, punished at Hell's depth, as it's peculiar to human beings, which means the most human part of this canticle is the most fraudulent.*

he was wrong. Wouldn't we gaze at beautiful horrors instead of trying to intervene? But we can't help ourselves, he thought.

Anne Agnes Dugas, considered a regionalist, also got hellish in her final series of paintings: charcoal fields, bones whitening the bleak expanse, and it's nothing really—can we be shocked anymore?—until you realize the remains look uncannily like a field of blanched wildflowers. My dad liked this one especially. See, he would say. We can't help ourselves.

This has been a book of fathers, it seems. My own grandpa, like Uless, left after farming cane for decades. He kept walking, and no one knew where he ended up. He didn't know how to write, so he couldn't even send a postcard. But Dad stayed until he couldn't.

I can't help myself. All of these men, gone, returning now in these pages. It's not an act of grace, not forgiveness. It's spring. My dad, too. Spring.

One evening, we marveled at the clouds, silent and then suddenly luminous. We had been riding in his red truck. My dad said it's not real, heat lightning. It's a myth that temperature could crackle with light. But it's pretty, prettier than the truth, he said. A good story.

I keep telling it.

—Gus

Il reviendra,
mon père reviendra.
—TRADITIONAL ACADIAN BALLAD

ACKNOWLEDGMENTS

I would like to thank the editors of these journals and magazines where earlier versions of these poems appeared: *American Poetry Review*, *New England Review*, *Kenyon Review*, *Harvard Advocate*, *Nashville Review*, *Willow Springs*, *Southampton Review*, *Dodge*, *Appalachian Review*, *Louisville Review*, *PANK*, *Permafrost Magazine*, *Bear Review*, and *Kindred*. Particular thanks to editors David Baker, Jennifer Chang, Elizabeth Scanlon, and Sarah Green. Rodney Jones and Gabrielle Bates, you have my gratitude and admiration unending. Tiana Nobile, thank you for the belief and encouragement. Zoe-Aline Howard, thank you—you've been essential in finding this book's audience. And to J. Bruce Fuller, my brilliant editor at TRP, I'm indebted always. To the whole of TRP, especially Charlie Tobin: thank you.

I'm also grateful for my partner and keenest editor, Shelby MacRae, along with Nicholas Comeaux and Chris Monier, my dedicated readers and friends. Without Dr. Monier, the Louisiana French would not be what it is in this collection. Thank you to Lindon Stall, Daniel Lassell, M. Cynthia Cheung, Robert Brunet, Justin Lacour, CC Molaison, Kate Youngblood, Nicholas Molbert, and E. M. Tran for the friendship and support—for always talking about books and craft. And to my children, Edith and Marcel, if you read this one day.

ABOUT THE AUTHOR

BURNSIDE SOLEIL grew up in a houseboat on the bayou but these days is a pilgrim in New Orleans. His work has appeared in *American Poetry Review*, *Kenyon Review*, *New England Review*, and elsewhere.

THE SABINE SERIES IN LITERATURE

Series Editor: J. Bruce Fuller

The Sabine Series in Literature highlights work by authors born in or working in Texas and/or Louisiana. There are no thematic restrictions; TRP seeks the best writing possible by authors from this unique region of the American South.

Books in this series:

No. 001—Cody Smith—*Gulf*

No. 002—David Armand—*The Lord's Acre*

No. 003—Ron Rozelle—*Leaving the Country of Sin*

No. 004—Collier Brown—*Scrap Bones*

No. 005—Esteban Rodríguez—*Lotería*

No. 006—Elizabeth Burk—*Unmoored*

No. 007—Cliff Hudder—*Sallowsfield*

No. 008—C. Prudence Arceneaux—*Proprioception*

No. 009—Cody Smith—*River Hymnal*

No. 010—David Middleton—*Time Will Tell: Collected Poems*

No. 011—Ron Rozelle—*The Windows of Heaven* (25th Anniversary Edition)

No. 012—David Armand—*Walk the Night*

No. 013—Burnside Soleil—*Berceuse Parish*